© Copyright 2023 - All rights reserved.

The contents of this book may not be reproduced, duplicated, or transmitted without direct written permission from the author. Under no circumstances will any legal responsibility or blame be held against the publisher for any reparation, damages, or monetary loss due to the information herein, either directly or indirectly.

This book is a work of fiction. Names, characters, and incidents are either the product of the author's imagination or are used fictitiously. Any resemblance to actual persons living or dead, business establishments, events, or locales is entirely coincidental.

Legal Notice: This book is Copyright protected. This is only for personal use. You cannot amend, distribute, sell, use, quote, or paraphrase any part of this book's content without the author's consent.

Disclaimer Notice: Please note the information contained within this document is for educational and entertainment purposes only. Every attempt has been made to provide accurate, up-to-date, reliable, and complete information. No warranties of any kind are expressed or implied. Readers acknowledge that the author is not rendering legal, financial, medical, or professional advice. The content of this book has been derived from various sources. Please consult a licensed professional before attempting any techniques outlined in this book.

By reading this document, the reader agrees that under no circumstances is the author responsible for any losses, direct or indirect, which are incurred as a result of the use of the information contained within this document, including, but not limited to, —errors, omissions, or inaccuracies. For information regarding permission, email the author at kisaboyun@gmail.com.

DEDICATION

In loving memory, my beloved cat Simit. And the parents who are sick of piled-up bedding screaming out at them from the laundry room.

Let me know what you think about this book, or see me write next by sending me an email at kisaboyun@gmail.com. I promise never to spam your inbox.

SUPA CAT AND THE BEDWETTER

YOU ARE NOT ALONE

A.S.K. AYNUR

It was nighttime.

As usual, Rescue, the Supa Cat, was just finishing his dinner.

When his bowl was clean, he wiped his whiskers and wandered over to his cat bed.

When he got there, he pressed the secret button under the cushion, walked onto the cat bed,
and disappeared underground.

That's right... his cat bed was the entrance to his secret lair... the Cat Cave.

The cat bed landed on the cave floor, and Rescue walked out into his lab.

Rescue's sidekick, Delilah the Dog, was sitting at a huge screen with lots of data on it.

'What have we got this evening Delilah?' asked Rescue.

'The sensor is picking up something from number 26,' said Delilah. 'Maybe you should check it out.'

'Thanks. I will,' said Rescue.

Rescue, as you may already know, was no ordinary cat.
But it wasn't just bravery and a Cat Cave that made him a Supa Cat.
He had powers too.

One of the powers he used most often was his Rescue Radar.
He could sense children that needed rescuing.
He could see into their minds to find out what they needed rescuing from.

Rescue closed his eyes and concentrated on the fear and worry coming from number 26, Paw Avenue.

In an instant, Rescue was seeing the world through the eyes of a young squirrel named Sybil. She seemed very anxious.

'What if I never learn not to wet the bed?' she wailed.

'Of course, you will,' said her mom, the Chipmunk.

'But I've been wetting the bed for months!' cried Sybil.

"I know it's hard," said her mom calmly. "But nothing lasts forever.

You just wait.

Be patient.

Because one day soon, as if by magic... you will wake up completely dry Patience, my love.

Now, off to bed."

'I've seen enough,' thought Rescue.
He opened his eyes.

'What was it, boss?' asked Delilah.
'Another bedwetter,' said Rescue.

'You'll have that sorted out in no time at all!' said Delilah.
'You bet,' said Rescue. 'Now... open the Dream Walker, would you?'
'Sure thing,' said Delilah, pressing a big blue button.

A helmet with hundreds of wires and tubes coming out of it came down from the ceiling. The Dream Walker was a machine of Rescue's own invention.

He used it to enter the dreams of children and save them from wetting their beds. Rescue put it on.

Down the road, at number 26, Sybil had just fallen asleep. She was dreaming about a tree full of acorns... her favorite food in the world.

Little did she know that pee was gathering up inside her, waiting to burst out.

Suddenly, in her dream, a cat fell out of the tree.

It wasn't just any cat, though.

It was Rescue.

Rescue walked over to Sybil and began to lick her face.

'Wait,' Sybil said in her dream. 'What are you doing?

STOP!

STOP THAT!

Why are you doing that?'

But Rescue didn't stop.

He licked harder and harder.

His rough tongue was like sandpaper against Sybil's skin.

'I don't like it!' screamed Sybil. 'Make it stop!
Wake up me!
WAKE UP!'

And just like that, Sybil's eyes sprang open.
'Well, that wasn't nice,' she thought.
'Wait... I need to pee.
That was good timing.
I would never have woken up if that cat hadn't come along!'

Sybil went off to the toilet.
She wasn't even a bit bothered about her weird dream because she was going to pee in the toilet... not in her bed.

Back in the lab, Rescue took off the Dream Walker.

"Mission accomplished?" asked Delilah.

"Another bedwetter rescued!" said Rescue.

"Awesome!" said Delilah.

The next morning, Sybil shot downstairs.

She was so excited.

'I did it. I DID IT!' she yelled.

'What did you do?' asked her mom.

'I'm dry. I didn't wet the bed!' said Sybil.

'That's amazing!' said her mom. 'Well done!'

'Thanks, Mom. I'm so happy,' said Sybil, giving her mom a big hug.

'You see, darling!' her mom said. 'Things always turn out OK in the end. You just have to be a little bit patient.'

About the Author

Accidental author A.S.K. Aynur holds a Forensic Medicine Cert., Cert. in Early Childhood Education & Care Competency, and a Diploma in Counselling.

She is also a Paediatric Hypnosis Coach, Parents Coach, Kids Coach, ICF Accredited Life Coach, and Speaker. Despite her struggles to read and not having the ambition to write as a child, she became a best-selling author in 2020 with her first book.

That she has many strings to her bow is no surprise to anybody who knows her, as she is a serial entrepreneur. She describes her mind as very active and uses writing to get her ideas out and focus her thoughts. Her inspirations come from far and wide. She looks to world events, real-life stories, personal experiences, and the work of other writers.

Through her writing, she hopes to impress on her readers that, whatever life throws at you, there is always a funny side. She also aims to help parents teach their children good values through entertaining tales.

www.ingramcontent.com/pod-product-compliance
Lightning Source LLC
Chambersburg PA
CBHW041504220426
43661CB00016B/1246